The
SMALL and MIGHTY
Book of
Sharks

Published in 2022 by OH!.
An imprint of Welbeck Children's Limited. part of Welbeck Publishing Group
Based in London and Sydney.

www.welbeckpublishing.com

A CIP catalogue record for this book is available from the Library of Congress.

Writer: Ben Hoare
Illustrator: Kirsti Davidson
Consultant: Stephen Savage
Design and text by Raspberry Books Ltd
Project Manager: Russell Porter
Editorial Manager: Joff Brown
Design Manager: Matt Drew
Production: Jess Brisley

ISBN 978 1 83935 194 5

Printed in Heshan. China

10 9 8 7 6 5 4 3 2 1

FSC
www.fsc.org
MIX
Paper from
responsible sources
FSC® C020056

The
SMALL and MIGHTY
Book of
Sharks

Ben Hoare and Kirsti Davidson

Contents

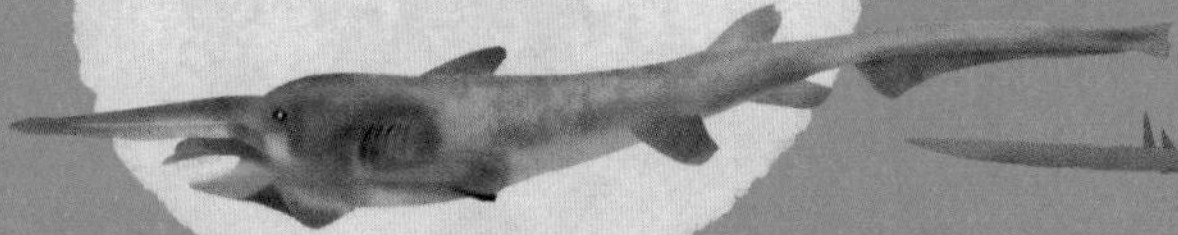

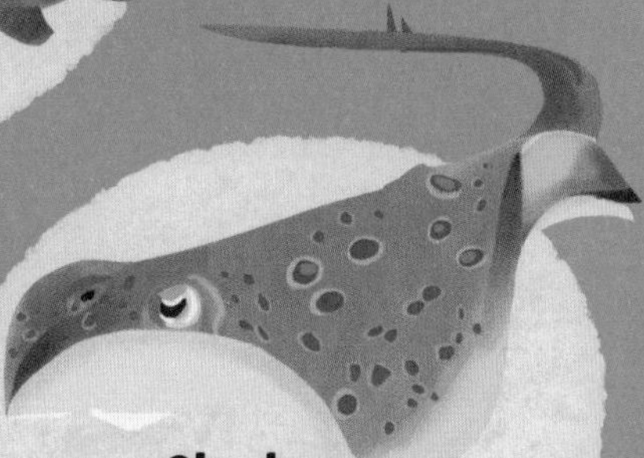

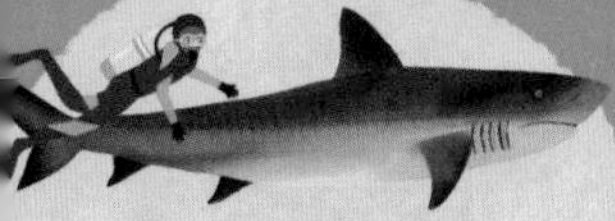

INTRODUCTION

This little book is absolutely bursting
with facts about sharks.

Sharks swim in all of the world's
seas. They come in many shapes
and sizes. Some are intelligent and
powerful hunters, but only a few are
dangerous to people.

There are sharks that . . .

grow as big as a bus
make friends with other sharks
give birth to hundreds of babies
glow in the dark.

Sharks are amazing!

Let's dive in and meet
some of them.

What are Sharks?

SHARKS

are an ancient group of fish.
They first appeared on Earth
around 450 million years ago.
That makes them much older
than the dinosaurs.

A gigantic shark called
MEGALODON
was the biggest fish that ever lived. "Meg" probably hunted whales and dolphins and had teeth as long as bananas. Some teeth survive as fossils.

Megalodon

SHARKS LIVE
anywhere in the ocean.

You'll find them at the **SUNLIT SURFACE**, all the way down to the **DEEPEST SEABED** where it is always **INKY-BLACK** and **COLD**. There are sharks in freezing Arctic seas, warm tropical seas, and everywhere in between.

There are
over **500**
species of
SHARK.

THE LARGEST SHARK ALIVE TODAY
(and the world's largest fish) is the whale shark. It grows up to 46 ft. long—as big as a bus. Its massive mouth is around 5 ft. from end to end—wide enough to swallow a person. Fortunately, this huge shark eats only small prey.

whale shark

The smallest shark is the
DWARF LANTERNSHARK,
which is just **8-10 IN. LONG.**

THE TOP 10 BIGGEST SHARKS ARE:

∽

1. Whale shark—46 ft.
2. Basking shark—36 ft.
3. Tiger shark—24 ft.
4=.Great white shark—21 ft.
4=.Greenland shark—21 ft.
6. Common thresher shark—19 ft.
7. Great hammerhead shark—18.5 ft.
8. Megamouth shark—18 ft.
9. Bull shark—11 ft.
10. Sand tiger shark—10.5 ft.

(These are their maximum sizes.)

tiger
shark

great
hammerhead
shark

whale
shark

17

SHARKS don't have bones.
Instead, their entire skeleton
is made from **CARTILAGE**.
It is strong, yet also light
and bendy. We have cartilage
too—for example, in our
ears and at the front
of our nose.

HAVING A LIGHT
AND FLEXIBLE
SKELETON MEANS
THAT MANY SHARKS
SWIM FAST AND CAN
STEER FAST TOO.

~

A **SHARK** HAS A

stiff fin on its back, called
the **dorsal fin.** This slides above
water when the shark swims
at the surface.

tail fins

Side fins give the shark lift, like the wings of an airplane. Strong tail fins sweep from side to side to power the shark forward.

dorsal fin

side fin

21

All fish have
SCALES,
but those of sharks are a bit
different. They are hard and
spiky, as if sharks are covered
in thousands of tiny teeth.
If you stroked a shark,
it would feel rough,
like sandpaper.

The tooth-like scales
help sharks swim faster. When
water flows over their body,
it doesn't slow them down
as much as ordinary
scales would.

pale belly

Many sharks are **dark on top** and **paler on their belly**. This is a clever camouflage that hides sharks from their prey. Here's how it works ...

When fish look down at a shark **swimming below them,** its dark back matches the darkness of the deep ocean. So the shark seems to disappear. When fish look up at the **shark from underneath,** its pale belly matches the bright sunlight at the ocean surface. Once again, the shark appears to vanish.

dark back

Most sharks are gray or brown,

but the lemon shark is yellowish and the blue shark is bluish. The leopard shark has handsome spots and the pyjama shark has stripes like a pair of stripy pajamas!

Every

WHALE
SHARK

has its own pattern of white spots.
Scientists photograph these patterns
to tell the sharks apart.

~

10 sharks named after other animals:

1. Bull shark
2. Cat shark
3. Cow shark
4. Crocodile shark
5. Leopard shark

~

6. Salmon shark
7. Tiger shark
8. Weasel shark
9. Whale shark
10. Zebra shark

A SHARK BREATHES THROUGH THE TALL SLITS
BEHIND ITS HEAD. THESE ARE GILLS.
USUALLY, THERE ARE FIVE OF THEM.

water with oxygen, in

water without
oxygen, out

Sharks swim with their mouths open.
Sea water flows in, and the gills take the
gas oxygen out of the water. Sharks, like all
animals, need oxygen to survive. The waste water
flows out again through the gill slits.

31

SHARKS ARE PREDATORS.

The shape of their teeth can give clues about their diet . . .

Flat, crunching teeth—perfect for crushing the shells of crabs and shellfish

Needle-like teeth—best for grabbing slippery squid and small fish

Sharp, saw-edged teeth —perfect for grabbing and slashing large prey

33

34

SHARKS have several rows of teeth.

Only the first two are used—the rest are waiting their turn. As teeth at the front fall out, new ones slide forward to replace them. Shark teeth don't have roots like ours do, so they fall out quite easily.

A great white shark has around 250 TEETH. But it will use, lose, and replace thousands in its lifetime! For a shark, the process of using, losing, and replacing teeth never stops.

Feeding
Time

SHARKS

FIND THEIR PREY
IN MANY WAYS:

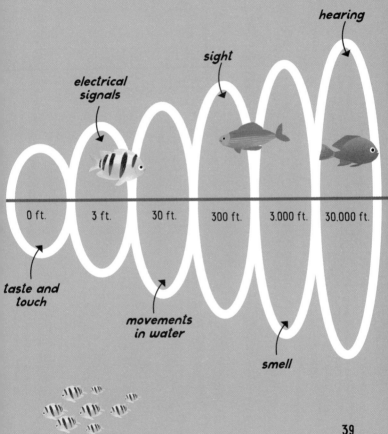

electrical
signals

sight

hearing

taste and
touch

movements
in water

smell

| 0 ft. | 3 ft. | 30 ft. | 300 ft. | 3.000 ft. | 30.000 ft. |

39

SHARKS HAVE EXCELLENT HEARING. THEY CAN HEAR THINGS IN THE WATER UP TO 3,300 FT. AWAY. THEY ARE ESPECIALLY GOOD AT HEARING THE SOUNDS MADE BY INJURED FISH AS THEY STRUGGLE OR PANIC.

A SHARK'S EARS ARE
JUST BEHIND ITS EYES.
THEY LOOK LIKE
LITTLE HOLES.

AS FAR AS WE KNOW,
SHARKS DON'T
MAKE ANY CALLS
OR SOUNDS.

~

SHARKS

CAN SEE COLORS BUT
CAN'T TELL THEM APART,
SO THEY ARE COLOR BLIND.
BUT IN DARK OR MURKY
WATER, THEIR EYESIGHT IS
MUCH BETTER THAN OURS.

WHEN SHARKS CHARGE AT PREY, THEIR EYES COULD BE DAMAGED. SO SOME SHARKS HAVE AN EXTRA EYELID ON EACH EYE. IT IS TOUGH AND CLOSES FOR PROTECTION AS THE SHARK ATTACKS. OTHER SHARKS ROLL THEIR EYES ALL THE WAY BACK INTO THEIR SOCKETS.

SHARKS smell a trail of blood left by prey. A **great white shark** could sniff a single drop of blood in a swimming pool!

UP TO **TWO-THIRDS** OF A SHARK'S **BRAIN** IS USED **JUST** FOR SMELL.

an adult shark's brain is shaped like this

The sides of a shark, from head to tail, are packed with movement sensors.

46

These notice any movements in the water. Sharks can feel the ripples made by fish 330 ft. away.

ALL ANIMALS CREATE
TINY AMOUNTS OF

ELECTRICITY

WHEN THEIR HEART PUMPS AND MUSCLES
MOVE. AMAZINGLY, SHARKS ARE ABLE
TO TUNE INTO THESE FAINT ELECTRICAL
SIGNALS GIVEN OFF BY OTHER
ANIMALS IN THE OCEAN.

A shark's nose has many little **freckles** or **dimples.** These are special cells filled with jelly-like fluid and linked to nerves. They are sensitive to electrical signals, so they give the shark its

ELECTROSENSE.

WHEN SOME LARGE SHARKS GET REALLY CLOSE, THEY BUMP THEIR PREY TO CHECK IT OUT. THEY MAY ALSO TAKE A QUICK BITE TO SEE IF IT TASTES GOOD. WHILE FEEDING, SHARKS SHAKE THEIR HEADS

VIOLENTLY.

THIS HELPS THEIR TEETH TO SLICE OFF CHUNKS OF FLESH. THEY CAN'T CHEW, SO THEY SWALLOW FOOD WHOLE.

SALMON SHARKS
are named after their
favorite food—salmon.

(But lemon sharks don't eat
lemons, and tiger sharks don't
eat tigers! These sharks get their
name from their appearance.)

Tiger sharks will eat anything meaty. They even hunt sea turtles and patrol beaches to catch seabird chicks taking their first flights. Clumsy birds that crash-land in the water need to watch out!

GREAT WHITE SHARKS

charge their prey
from below to take
it by surprise.

GREAT WHITE SHARK MENU:

~

1. large fish such as tuna
2. seals
3. sea lions
4. porpoises
5. dolphins
6. other sharks

Some sharks hunt in groups.

They power into a shoal of fish, which panic and bunch up. This is called a bait ball. Now the sharks attack from all sides.

On the coast of South Africa, **copper sharks** team up with dolphins to round up fish together.

SPINNER SHARKS leap out of the water as they target shoals of fish. They spin in the air up to three times.

ANGEL SHARKS LIE IN WAIT FOR PREY. WITH A WIDE, FLAT BODY, THEY ARE BEAUTIFULLY **CAMOUFLAGED** AGAINST THE SANDY SEABED. THE **PERFECT AMBUSH.**

plankton

BASKING
SHARKS

are the world's **second largest fish**, after whale
sharks. Both these giants feed on **plankton.**
They glide along with their cave-like jaws open wide and
in flow mighty mouthfuls of plankton-rich water.

60

PLANKTON INCLUDES THE
TINY EGGS AND YOUNG OF
MANY SEA CREATURES, SUCH AS:

1. shrimps
2. jellyfish
3. crabs
4. starfish
5. fish

~ SLEEPER ~
SHARKS

patrol the bottom of the ocean.

Food down here is difficult to find, so
they swim very slowly to save energy.
Perhaps you can see how they
got their name?

THE BODY OF A
DEAD WHALE
THAT HAS SUNK TO THE SEABED IS

A WELCOME FEAST FOR

DEEP-SEA
SHARKS

~

Different sharks swim at

DIFFERENT
DEPTHS

in the ocean.

TYPE OF SHARK	DEEPEST THEY SWIM
REEF SHARK, BULL SHARK, NURSE SHARK	100 FT.
WHALE SHARK	330 FT.
BASKING SHARK	660 FT.
GREAT WHITE SHARK	1,150 FT.
TIGER SHARK	2,460 FT.
SLEEPER SHARK	100 FT.
COOKIECUTTER SHARK	3,300 FT.

Sometimes sharks
like to eat . . .
OTHER SHARKS!
Bigger sharks are a
constant danger to
small sharks that are
still growing up.

Even the strongest, fastest and fiercest sharks HAVE PREDATORS. Great white sharks are hunted by groups of ORCAS.

↑
orca

Cool Things Sharks Do

Many sharks feed at night.

So . . . what do sharks do during the day?
They take a rest. But they're not sleeping
the way we do. It's more like dozing
gently but with their eyes open!

THESE ARE THE TOP SPEEDS OF THE THREE FASTEST SHARKS (THEY CAN ONLY SWIM THIS FAST IN SHORT BURSTS):

1. Mako shark 31 mph
—top speed of a grizzly bear running

2. Salmon shark 28 mph
   —record set by Usain Bolt,
   the fastest-ever human sprinter

**3. Great white
   shark 22 mph**
   —the fastest a Nile
   crocodile can swim

We say sharks are

"COLD-BLOODED"

because their body is usually the same temperature as the sea. But a few sharks can take heat from their muscles to superheat their body. Parts of their body become several degrees warmer than the water around them— useful for chilly seas!

salmon shark

SALMON SHARKS AND **GREAT WHITE SHARKS** CAN DO THIS.

great white shark

EARTH IS LIKE A GIANT MAGNET. Sharks can feel its invisible pull. They can tell which way is north and which is south. This magnetic supersense helps them find their way across the ocean.

green turtle

wandering albatross

Sharks aren't the only animals with this ability. Salmon, sea turtles, and many birds have it too.

Atlantic salmon

Arctic tern

77

Some sharks make long journeys called migrations.

SCALLOPED HAMMERHEAD SHARKS

swim to the middle of the Pacific Ocean, where they swarm around seamounts, which are undersea mountains. We're not sure why, but it could be to breed.

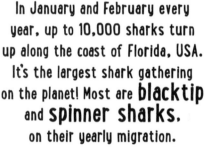

In January and February every year, up to 10,000 sharks turn up along the coast of Florida, USA. It's the largest shark gathering on the planet! Most are **blacktip** and **spinner sharks,** on their yearly migration. Some come within a stone's throw of the beach.

79

Most sharks hang out near the shore
or around coral reefs. However,
BLUE SHARKS
cruise the ocean, hundreds of miles
from land. They sometimes chase
prey in packs, like wolves.

BULL SHARKS

can survive in fresh water, so they can swim up rivers. Young ones are often spotted in the river that runs though the Australian city of Brisbane! There were sharks living in the river long before the city existed.

Many sharks live on their own
most of the time, but they
can be social too.

GRAY REEF SHARKS

seem to make friends. They
form groups that get together
each morning and evening.
Perhaps they're sharing
information about good
places to find food?
No one knows.

REMORAS

are fish that hitch a lift on sharks. A sucker on their head lets them cling on, so they can grab scraps of food the sharks miss as well as dead skin and parasites. As the sharks are not hurt, they don't mind.

remora fish

Believe it or not, sharks can have **DIFFERENT PERSONALITIES.** Shark researchers have found that some are **CURIOUS** and **PLAYFUL,** some are **BOLD** and **TAKE RISKS,** and others are **NERVOUS.**

Most species of shark give birth to live babies, or pups. The record is held by whale shark moms, **which have around 300 pups.** Other sharks release eggs that develop outside the mother.

Baby sand tiger sharks may eat one another inside their mother, before even being born. The larger, stronger babies **eat their smaller brothers and sisters**. Only one or two pups survive to be born.

Catsharks produce mysterious egg cases known as mermaid's purses. These are leathery pouches that the female catshark lays among seaweed. Inside each pouch is a baby shark. It spends 7–10 months growing, then the egg case splits open and it hatches.

Empty mermaid's purses wash up on beaches. Keep an eye out for them!

BULLHEAD SHARKS AND **PORT JACKSON SHARKS** LAY EGGS WITH EGG CASES SHAPED LIKE CORKSCREWS. THE MOTHER SHARK WEDGES HER EGGS INTO A CRACK IN A ROCK UNDERWATER SO IT DOESN'T DRIFT AWAY.

89

Weird and Wonderful Sharks

HAMMERHEAD SHARKS

have a T-shaped head with an eye at each end.

It gives the shark all-around vision and seems to work like a scanner on the seabed. As the shark turns its head left and right, it covers a large area of the seabed and picks up a lot of information about its prey using its electrical sense.

93

The

BONNETHEAD SHARK

eats plants! Scientists discovered that it grazes seagrass, which forms green meadows on the seabed. But it hunts prey too.

The
EPAULETTE SHARK

is often called the "walking shark" because it can **crawl out of water.** Using its fins as feet, it wriggles over coral reefs and rocks at low tide. This helps it reach parts of the reef other sharks can't get to. After catching crabs on the reef, it returns to the sea.

95

GOBLIN SHARKS
HAVE A BIZARRE NOSE
"HORN." IT IS FULL OF
ELECTRICAL SENSORS,
SO IT HELPS THEM FIND
PREY IN THEIR DARK,
DEEP-SEA HOME. THESE
STRANGE SHARKS
ARE ALSO PINK!

THE COOKIECUTTER SHARK

is no bigger than a pet cat. At night,
the little shark swims up to other fish
and clamps on with its strong mouth.
Next it spins around to rip off a
small chunk of flesh, leaving
a cookie-shaped hole.

There's no doubt which sharks have the longest tail. In

THRESHER SHARKS,

it can be up to 10 ft. long. They use their incredible tail like a whip, to round up fish and lash them. The wounded fish can't escape and are easy for the thresher sharks to catch.

MOST GREENLAND SHARKS CAN'T SEE A
THING. A PARASITE LIVES ON THEIR EYEBALL,
MAKING THEM BLIND. DESPITE THIS, THEY
HAVE NO PROBLEM FINDING FOOD.

GREENLAND SHARKS ARE FOUND IN DEEP,
ICE-COLD ARCTIC SEAS. THEY TAKE EVERYTHING
SLOWLY AND DON'T BECOME ADULTS UNTIL
THEY'RE 150 YEARS OLD. SOME GET TRULY
ANCIENT AND LIVE LONGER THAN ANY
OTHER FISH IN THE WORLD
—UP TO 400 YEARS.

The brilliant white teeth of the

FRILLED SHARK

would impress any dentist. They're
white for a deadly reason—to
attract small fish and squid,
which swim up for a closer
look. Big mistake!

THE PORT JACKSON SHARK
MIGHT WIN THE PRIZE OF
ODDEST-LOOKING SHARK.
IT HAS AN UNUSUAL DIET TOO—
PRICKLY SEA URCHINS. THESE
LOOK LIKE UNDERWATER
HEDGEHOGS. BUT ARE
NO MATCH FOR THE
SHARK'S CRUSHING TEETH.

CAN YOU TELL HOW THE
LONGNOSE SAWSHARK
GETS A MEAL? THE FRONT OF ITS HEAD IS
SUPER-STRETCHED AND SHARP TEETH STICK
OUT DOWN THE EDGES. IT'S LIKE HAVING
A CHAINSAW ON YOUR HEAD!
TO KILL FISH, ALL THE SAWSHARK HAS
TO DO IS SWING ITS HEAD SIDEWAYS.

Lanternsharks live in the deep sea and glow in the dark! Special organs light up their bodies like fairy lights. This tempts prey closer.

Weirdly, it also hides the lanternsharks. Their glow matches the faint light coming from way up above, so it hides these little sharks from their enemies.

CATSHARKS

don't look like cats, but their eyes do look like cats' eyes. They are large and oval—surprisingly cat-like.

Some catsharks curl up into a ball if they are caught. They cover their head with their tail, as if trying to hide! Some types of catshark are also called shysharks.

A

WOBBEGONG

has wavy flaps of skin around
its huge head. It looks more like
a seaweedy rock than a shark.
When it lies on the bottom, other
fish have no idea it's there. If
they swim in range, it rockets up
to snatch them.

When the wobbegong opens its wide mouth, it creates so much suction, **prey is slurped up instantly.** Often the shark gulps down fish and crabs whole.

MEGAMOUTH SHARKS

ARE ENORMOUS—ABOUT THE SIZE
OF A MINIBUS—YET HAVE HARDLY
EVER BEEN SEEN. FEWER THAN 100
OF THESE GIANTS HAVE BEEN
RECORDED. WE KNOW THEY HOOVER
UP SMALL PREY BY SWIMMING WITH
THEIR JAWS OPEN, BUT ALMOST
EVERYTHING ELSE ABOUT THEM IS
A MYSTERY. THERE'S SO MUCH STILL
TO DISCOVER ABOUT SHARKS . . .

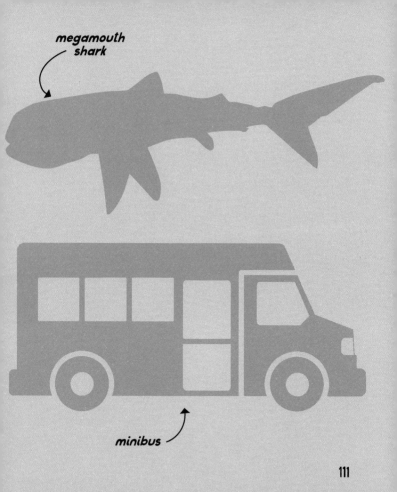

megamouth
shark

minibus

111

Skates
and
Rays

Two other groups of fish, the **SKATES AND RAYS,** are close relatives of sharks and have a lot in common with them. Like sharks, they have a skeleton made of cartilage. **ALSO LIKE SHARKS, THESE ARE ANCIENT CREATURES THAT HAVE NOT CHANGED MUCH FOR MILLIONS OF YEARS.**

SOME FEATURES OF SKATES AND RAYS:

- A FLAT BODY
- MOUTH ON THE UNDERSIDE
- CARTILAGE SKELETON
- TWO SIDE FINS SHAPED LIKE WINGS
- A LONG, THIN TAIL.

115

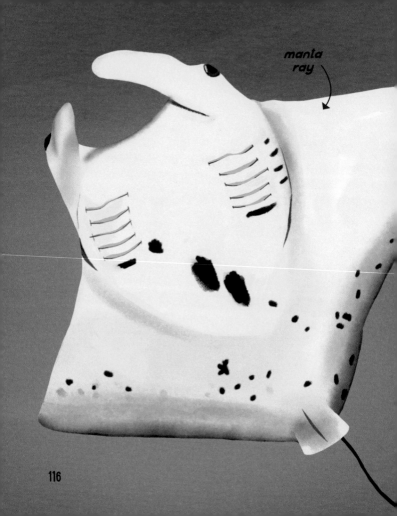

manta ray

Large numbers of skates are caught for food. Due to years of fishing, the **FLAPPER SKATE** is now more **ENDANGERED** than the blue whale or the giant panda.

Skates have an unusual, diamond-shaped body.

Most skates and rays live on or near the seabed, where their flattened body comes in very useful. When resting on the bottom, they breathe in through openings on top of their head. They breathe out through **gills, which are underneath.**

THE
OCEANIC MANTA

IS THE LARGEST RAY IN
THE WORLD. AS IT CRUISES
THROUGH THE WATER, IT
FLAPS ITS MASSIVE SIDE
FINS LIKE A FLYING BIRD.
PRONGS IN FRONT OF THE
MANTA'S HEAD PUSH FOOD
INTO ITS MOUTH.

MANTAS HAVE THE **BIGGEST BRAIN** OF ANY FISH. THEY ARE GENTLE WITH DIVERS AND SEEM TO ENJOY SWIMMING WITH PEOPLE.

THE **BLUE-SPOTTED STINGRAY** LIVES ON CORAL REEFS. ITS BEAUTIFUL SPOTS ARE A WARNING THAT IT HAS A SECRET WEAPON: **VENOMOUS SPINES ON THE TAIL.** THESE ARE NOT FOR ATTACKING PREY BUT FOR DEFENSE. IF SOMETHING DISTURBS THE STINGRAY, ITS SPINES CAN DELIVER A PAINFUL WOUND.

During the day, **MANY SKATES AND RAYS REST ON THE BOTTOM** and bury themselves in sand. Often just their eyes and tail are showing.

Part of the sea near Grand Cayman, an island in the Caribbean, is known as

STINGRAY CITY.

Every day, dozens of southern stingrays gather here in the warm, shallow water to be fed by tourists.

SPOTTED EAGLE RAYS

get together in groups, or schools. In a big school there can be several hundred rays.

MOBULA RAYS

make spectacular leaps right out of
the sea. They belly-flop back in with
a splash that can be seen and felt
far away. It is likely to be a
way of attracting mates.

Electric rays have a pair of
organs that produce—maybe
you can guess?—

ELECTRICITY.

In some species,

THE SHOCK

can be as much as

220 VOLTS

That's enough to give you a
serious jolt. No wonder they
are also called crampfish!
The rays use their electric
shock to stun prey and
their enemies.

Sharks
and
People

Sharks have a bad
reputation for attacking
humans, but they don't deserve
it. On average each year, sharks
**KILL JUST SIX OR SEVEN
PEOPLE WORLDWIDE.**
More people die from
LIGHTNING STRIKES
or by having accidents
while taking selfies!

COUNTRIES WITH THE MOST SHARK DEATHS:

1. USA
2. Australia
3. South Africa
4. Brazil
5. New Zealand

MOST SHARKS ARE HARMLESS
AND MORE AFRAID OF US THAN
WE ARE OF THEM. ONLY A FEW
SPECIES ARE EVER LIKELY TO
ATTACK. WHEN THEY DO, IT IS
ALMOST ALWAYS BECAUSE THEY
HAVE MISTAKEN US FOR THEIR
USUAL PREY. TO A SHARK,
A SURFBOARD AND SURFER
CAN LOOK LIKE A SEAL.

What to do if a shark
comes near you:

DON'T:
panic, splash around,
or make lots of noise

DO:
stay calm until it leaves

~

THE GREATEST THREAT TO SHARKS IS . . . US.

We are emptying the ocean of sharks. It is thought that we kill as many as

100 MILLION SHARKS

each year. More than one in ten shark species are at risk of dying out, or going extinct.

MANY SHARKS ARE

CAUGHT BY ACCIDENT.

THEY DIE IN NETS OR ON HOOKED

LINES PUT OUT FOR OTHER

FISH, SUCH AS TUNA. THIS IS

A TERRIBLE WASTE, AS THE DEAD

SHARKS ARE THROWN BACK

INTO THE SEA. SHARKS ARE

ALSO CAUGHT FOR THEIR MEAT.

In parts of Asia, shark fins are used
to make soup. Shark-fin soup
is now banned in
some countries.

There is plenty of
good news about sharks.
If we stop fishing them, their
populations recover. When
fishing stopped at a marine
reserve in the Pacific Ocean,
the number of sharks there
went up 2,000 times
in six years!

Today, there are
SHARK SANCTUARIES
all over the world. Tourists visit
to go shark-watching and
you can sometimes swim
with the sharks.

People on the Hawaiian islands used to worship sharks as gods. The most powerful shark god was the mighty

KAMOHOALIʻI,

who had a magical ability to turn into any other fish. Hawaiian people also thought that when they died, their bodies transformed into sharks. They believed that the shark spirits of their ancestors would protect them.

IN THE SEAS AROUND INDONESIA,

WHALE SHARKS

HAVE LEARNED THAT SOME FISHING
BOATS OFFER AN EASY MEAL. THEY
SWIM BESIDE THE BOATS AND RUB
AGAINST THE SIDES TO ASK FOR FOOD.
THE FISHERS ALLOW THE FRIENDLY
SHARKS TO TAKE SOME OF
THEIR CATCH.

Scientists tag sharks to see where they go and learn more about their lives. The tags weigh only as much as a bar of chocolate, and attach to the dorsal fin. They send radio signals when the sharks are at the surface, so the team on land can track their movements.

RECORD SHARK JOURNEYS, ALL MORE THAN 12,500 MI.:

NICOLE, FEMALE GREAT WHITE SHARK—FROM AFRICA TO AUSTRALIA AND BACK AGAIN

ANNE, FEMALE WHALE SHARK—ACROSS THE PACIFIC OCEAN

HELL'S BAY, MALE MAKO SHARK—ACROSS THE ATLANTIC OCEAN

141

142

SHARKS, SKATES, AND RAYS

ARE SOME OF THE MOST BEAUTIFUL AND EXCITING FISH IN THE SEA. LET'S ALL TAKE GOOD CARE OF THEM, SO THEY CAN LIVE THEIR LIVES IN PEACE.

143